CW00642508

RAILWAY HISTORY IN PICTURES

THE LANCASHIRE & YORKSHIRE RAILWAY

John Marshall

DAVID & CHARLES
NEWTON ABBOT LONDON NORTH POMFRET (VT) VANCOUVER

ISBN 0 7153 7478 8
Library of Congress Catalog Card Number 77-89516

Photoset and Printed in Great Britain
by Redwood Burn, Trowbridge & Esher
for David & Charles (Publishers) Limited
Brunel House Newton Abbot Devon

Published in the United States of America
by David & Charles Inc
North Pomfret Vermont 05053 USA

Published in Canada
by Douglas David & Charles Limited
1875 Welch Street North Vancouver BC

Contents

Frontispiece and Jacket: An Aspinall 4–4–2 on the 14.45 Manchester–Blackpool train at Bolton on 21 August 1907. (*National Railway Museum, York*)

Introduction

This collection of photographs portrays the many facets of the Lancashire & Yorkshire Railway and complements the three volume history of the L&Y published by David & Charles in 1969–72. In selecting the illustrations for the history many interesting pictures had to be omitted, and these form a large portion of this 'fourth volume'. Most of the photographs thus carry a volume and page reference to the history. Some were official LYR photographs copied from albums of prints at Horwich. For this facility I am grateful to British Rail Engineering Limited and to Mr G Drinkwater, former chief draughtsman at Horwich. Unfortunately many of the most interesting of these prints were too faded and discoloured to make reproducible copies. Others are from the Locomotive & General Railway Photographs collection for which I am grateful to the publishers, David & Charles, and others are from my own files. As much historical matter as possible has been included in the captions so that the book will form a useful adjunct to the history but will also stand on its own.

A BRIEF HISTORY OF THE RAILWAY

The Lancashire & Yorkshire Railway, with a total route mileage of 601 (967km) ranked eleventh in size of the principal British railway systems. Of these, however, it was the most complex, with a traffic density indicated by its final locomotive stock of 1650, exceeded only by the LNWR, GWR, Midland and NER, all of which operated from three to five times the mileage. Besides an intensive passenger traffic – in 1919 there were 79,119,010 passenger journeys – it carried an immense tonnage of coal and general merchandise, largely connected with the textile industries on both sides of the Pennines.

Its earliest section was the Manchester & Bolton Railway, opened on 29 May 1838, and built by the Manchester, Bolton & Bury Canal Navigation whose canal system was opened in 1800–5. What was always referred to as the 'main line' of the LYR, the Manchester & Leeds was opened throughout on 1 March 1841 from Manchester to Normanton. Here it joined the North Midland Railway whose tracks it used to Leeds. Engineering works included Summit tunnel between Littleborough and Todmorden, 2885yd and the longest on the LYR, and several other considerable tunnels on the Yorkshire side. It also gave access to York over the York & North Midland Railway opened on the same day as the North Midland Railway, 30 June 1840.

By a link from the Y&NM to the Leeds & Selby Railway (opened 23 September 1834) and the Hull & Selby (opened 1 July 1840) through railway communication was gained between Manchester and Hull. The gap in Manchester between the Oldham Road terminus of the Manchester & Leeds and the Liverpool Road terminus of the Liverpool & Manchester was all that prevented through communication between Liverpool and Hull. After prolonged arguments a connection was established from the M&L at Miles Platting, about ½ mile out of the terminus, down an incline to a central station, named Victoria, opened on 1 January 1844. The L&M built its connection from Ordsall Lane, again just short of its terminus, past the Salford terminus of the Manchester & Bolton Railway, and opened to Victoria on 4 May 1844.

Meanwhile, beyond Preston, the Preston & Wyre Railway had opened from Preston to Fleetwood on 16 July 1840 and, with the opening of the Bolton & Preston Railway throughout from Bolton to Euxton Junction on the North Union (Preston & Wigan) line on 22 June 1843, a through route was established from Manchester to Fleetwood.

For a period Fleetwood, named after its founder Peter Hesketh Fleetwood, formed the northern terminus of the route from London to Scotland and there were sailings from there to the Clyde. In 1846 the Preston & Wyre opened a branch to Blackpool which, thanks to the railway, developed from a small hamlet to a large resort.

The opening of the Bolton & Preston gave rise to a battle of fares with the North Union, brought to an end in 1844 by their amalgamation. The NUR was in turn leased jointly by the Grand Junction and Manchester & Leeds railways from 1 January 1846. The GJR became part of the London & North Western Railway on the formation of that company on 16 July 1846, and a month later, on 18 August, the Manchester & Bolton was amalgamated with the Manchester & Leeds.

From 1830 the Liverpool & Manchester and its successor, the LNWR, had had a monopoly of rail transport at Liverpool. In 1845 this was threatened by a new company, the Liverpool & Bury, promoting a line from Liverpool to Wigan, Bolton and Bury. This was taken over by the Manchester & Leeds and opened on 20 November 1848. At Bury it joined an extension of the former M&L Heywood branch, so making a through link to Rochdale.

Another important section of the system was the East Lancashire Railway consisting of lines from Clifton Junction, on the Manchester & Bolton Railway, to Bury and Rawtenstall, opened on 28 September 1846, extended to Bacup in 1848–52 and from near Ramsbottom to Accrington on 17 August 1848. At Accrington it branched eastwards to Burnley and Colne, completed in 1848–9, and westwards to Blackburn, 1848. Here it joined the Blackburn & Preston Railway, opened 1 June 1846 and two months later absorbed by the ELR. An extension to Liverpool from south of Preston, opened on 2 April 1849, was also absorbed by the ELR in 1846.

With its influence extending from Fleetwood to beyond Wakefield, the Manchester & Leeds, no doubt stimulated by the formation of the LNWR, changed its name to the Lancashire & Yorkshire Railway by Act of Parliament on 9 July 1847. At the same time it absorbed the Wakefield, Pontefract & Goole, opened on 29 March 1848, and the Ashton, Stalybridge & Liverpool Junction Railway, opened from Miles Platting to Stalybridge on 5 October 1846.

The Wakefield, Pontefract & Goole now established the LYR as a power on the East Coast and in due course the company was operating ships to the major North Sea ports in Denmark, Germany, Holland and Belgium. The LYR in fact became the largest ship owner of all the British railway companies. On the West Coast, L&Y ships operated between Fleetwood and Belfast, and between Liverpool and Drogheda.

The branch of the WP&G from Knottingley to Askern made an end-on junction with the Great Northern Railway at its northern terminus 'in a ploughed field four miles north of Doncaster' (to quote Edmund Denison, the GNR chairman). Another WP&G branch from Pontefract to Methley on the North Midland gave the GNR access to Leeds by running powers over the L&Y and Midland.

George Hudson's empire based on York was now being threatened by the northward drive of the GNR, and by a York & North Midland branch from Burton Salmon to Knottingley GNR trains could reach York by running powers over the L&Y and Y&NM. This and the Methley branch were opened in 1850.

Another LYR branch in this area was the Wakefield–Barnsley, opened on 1 January 1850. With a branch from collieries at Silkstone it was soon bringing immense quantities of coal onto the Goole line and in a few years its single line had to be doubled, though the second tunnel at Woolley was not built until 1900. With a length of 1745yd they ranked third in length on the LYR.

Other Yorkshire lines were the branch from the Manchester & Leeds to Halifax, opened on 1 July 1844, and the branch from Heaton Lodge to Huddersfield opened on 2 August 1847 as part of the LNWR. In 1849 this became part of the LNWR route from Stalybridge to Leeds giving a much more direct line from Manchester to Leeds using the LYR Stalybridge branch.

An isolated section of the LYR, from Huddersfield to the Manchester, Sheffield & Lincolnshire Railway at Penistone, with a branch to Holmfirth, was opened on 1 July 1850 and provided a new route from Sheffield to the north. Another branch from near Huddersfield to Meltham was opened in 1869. The Penistone line is the most scenic on the LYR system and includes some of the greatest engineering works, with immense viaducts at Lockwood, Denby Dale and Penistone, and several long tunnels. The Denby Dale viaduct was originally a timber trestle, replaced by the present stone structure in 1880.

More big viaducts and long tunnels had to be built on the extension of the LYR from Halifax to Bradford, with a 'short cut' from Sowerby Bridge, and another line from Mirfield to Low Moor. This last was opened on 12 July 1848. The extension to Bradford through Bowling tunnel, 1648yd, was not opened until 9 May 1850. Low Moor to Halifax, opened on 7 August 1850, included long tunnels at Wyke and Halifax and a 114ft (34.75m) high viaduct. The Halifax–Sowerby Bridge line, with another tunnel and viaduct, was opened on 1 January 1852. At last the LYR had a reasonable route

Above and Jacket: A scene on Accrington station, with a train from Burnley in the Blackburn line platform, on 3 June 1914. (Vol 1 p 112)
(*National Railway Museum, York*)

from Manchester to Bradford, but many years were to pass before a good service of express trains was established.

From Bowling Junction at the north end of Bowling tunnel above Bradford a line was built to Leeds by the Leeds, Bradford & Halifax Junction Co, later part of the GNR, and was opened on 1 August 1854, providing access for LYR trains to Leeds by running powers. Trains between Manchester, Leeds and Bradford were divided or combined at Low Moor or Halifax.

In Lancashire during this period the LYR had been expanding apace. The gap between Bolton and Blackburn was filled by the Blackburn, Darwen & Bolton Railway, opened on 12 June 1848. This included Sough tunnel, 2015yd, second longest on the LYR, and large viaducts near Entwistle and Bolton. It was extended northwards to Clitheroe and Chatburn on 21 June 1850. The Blackburn Co as it became known was a victim of the rivalry between the LYR and ELR which between them practically strangled it until, in 1857, it was forced into a joint amalgamation with the two companies.

On the Lancashire coast an important line was the Liverpool, Crosby & Southport, partly opened on 24 July 1848 and to Southport Chapel Street on 22 August 1851. It was amalgamated with the LYR on 1 January 1855. Shortly afterwards, on 9 April 1855, a railway was opened from Wigan to Southport by the LYR, though the section from Burscough to Southport was owned jointly by the LYR and ELR. These companies were also joint owners of the section from Walton Junction to Liverpool and from Clifton Junction to Salford. Amalgamation of the LYR and ELR, bitterly opposed and delayed by the Midland and LNWR, took place on 13 August 1859.

An early branch of the Manchester & Leeds, opened on 31 March 1842, left the main line near Middleton and after clambering up a half-mile incline at 1 in 27, terminated at Werneth on the outskirts of Oldham. On 1 November 1847 it was extended through two tunnels into the middle of Oldham at Mumps which remained the terminus until a further extension was opened to Rochdale on 2 November 1863 with a branch to

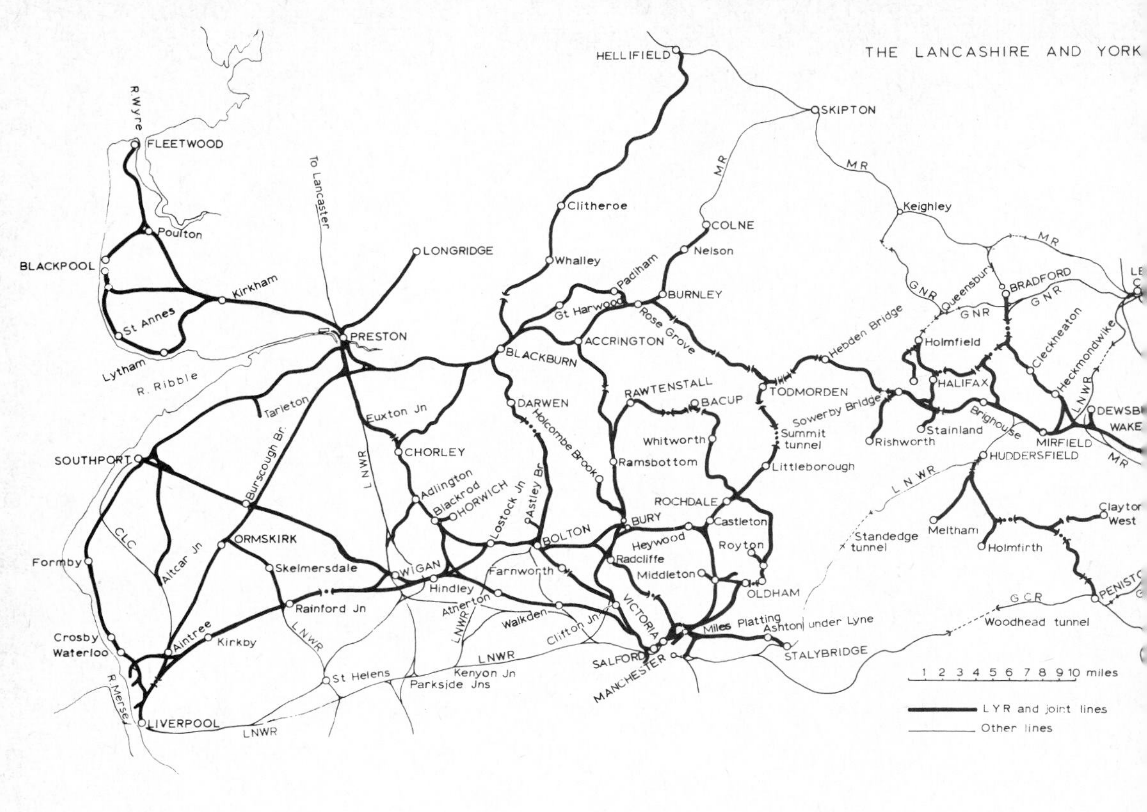
THE LANCASHIRE AND YORK
HELLIFIELD
SKIPTON
R Wyre
FLEETWOOD
To Lancaster
MR
MR
Keighley
Poulton
Clitheroe
COLNE
Nelson
MR
LONGRIDGE
BLACKPOOL
Whalley
Padiham
BURNLEY
Queensbury
BRADFORD
GNR
GNR
GNR
Kirkham
Gt Harwood
Rose Grove
St Annes
PRESTON
ACCRINGTON
Hebden Bridge
Holmfield
Cleckheaton
Heckmondwike
Lytham
BLACKBURN
R. Ribble
RAWTENSTALL
TODMORDEN
HALIFAX
LNWR
Tarleton
DARWEN
BACUP
Sowerby Bridge
DEWSB
Euxton Jn
Holcombe Brook
Summit tunnel
Brighouse
WAKE
SOUTHPORT
CHORLEY
Whitworth
Stainland
Rishworth
MIRFIELD
Burscough Br
L NWR
Ramsbottom
Littleborough
HUDDERSFIELD
MR
Adlington
Blackrod
HORWICH
Lostock Jn
Astley Br
L N WR
ROCHDALE
Claytor West
CLC
BURY
Castleton
Meltham
ORMSKIRK
BOLTON
Heywood
Standedge tunnel
Royton
Holmfirth
Formby
Altcar Jn
Radcliffe
Skelmersdale
WIGAN
Farnworth
Middleton
OLDHAM
PENISTO
Hindley
GCR
Rainford Jn
Atherton
VICTORIA
Crosby
Aintree
Walkden
Clifton Jn
Miles Platting
Ashton under Lyne
Woodhead tunnel
Waterloo
Kirkby
LNWR
LNWR
LNWR
SALFORD
STALYBRIDGE
R. Mersey
St Helens
Kenyon Jn
MANCHESTER
1 2 3 4 5 6 7 8 9 10 miles
Parkside Jns
LYR and joint lines
LIVERPOOL
Other lines
LNWR

R Wyre
FLEETWOOD
To Lancaster, Carlisle
Poulton
BLACKPOOL
North
South
Kirkham
St Annes
PRESTON
BLACKBURN
Lytham
R. Ribble
Euxton Jn
DARWEN
Sough tunnel
Chorley
SOUTHPORT
Adlington
Blackrod
Horwich works
Lostock Jn
Crow Nest Jn
BOLTON
ORMSKIRK
Formby
WIGAN
Farnworth
Hindley
Atherton
Walkden
Crosby
Aintree
Kirkby
Waterloo
St Helens
R. Mersey
LIVERPOOL
To London Euston

LWAY 1921

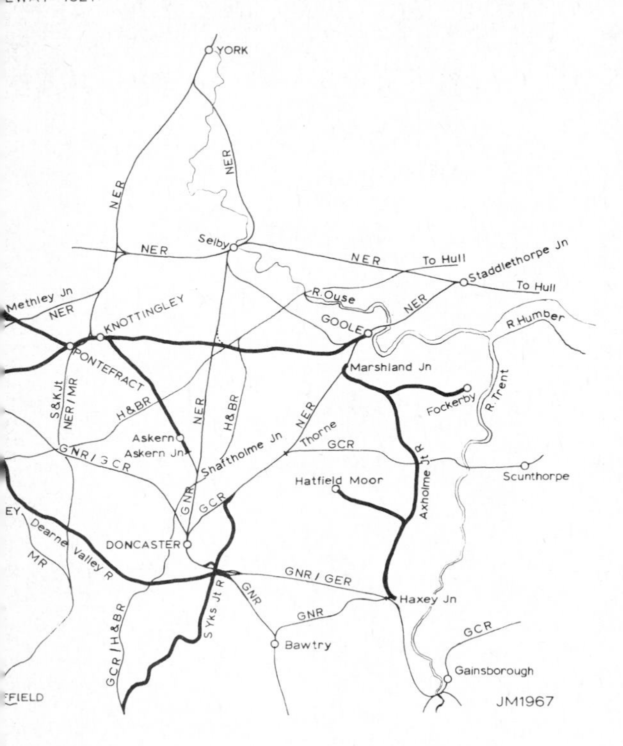

THE LANCASHIRE & YORKSHIRE SYSTEM IN 1977

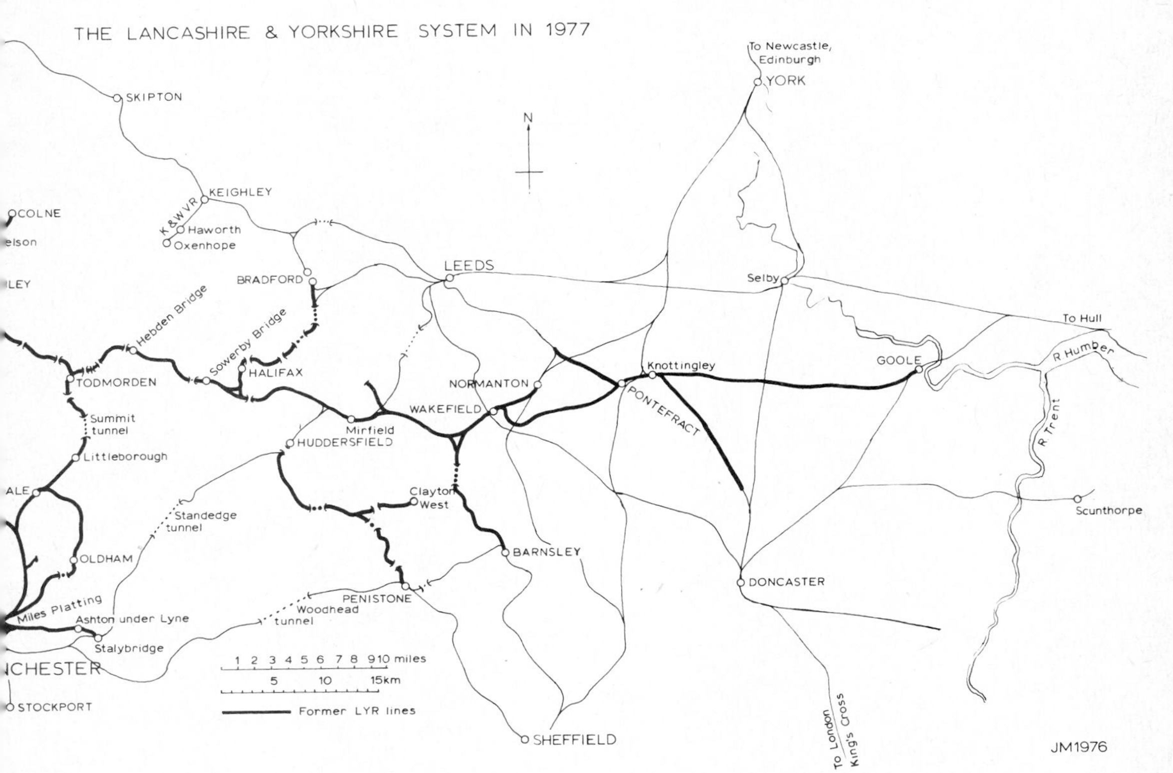

Above and Jacket: The LYR hauled an immense tonnage of coal in trains of up to 60 wagons, mostly privately owned. Here is one such train passing westwards through Horbury behind Aspinall 0–8–0 No 79. This engine, built in 1907 and scrapped in 1932, in common with most other members of its class, had a comparatively short life, largely because of inadequate bearings and faulty balancing. *(Locomotive & General Railway Photographs)*

Royton opened on 21 March 1864. In the same area a branch was opened from Middleton Junction down to Middleton on 5 January 1857.

Another important branch from the main line at Todmorden climbed through the Cliviger Gorge to a summit at Copy Pit and down to the ELR at Burnley. It was opened on 12 November 1849 and provided a useful route between Yorkshire and the Fylde coast beyond Preston.

The late 1860s and early 1870s saw the LYR at its lowest ebb. Shareholders were happy enough, for dividends were high, but this was largely because so little was being spent on improving the railway. Trains were slow, locomotives were of inadequate design and badly maintained, stations and carriages were in a decrepit state. From the mid 1870s a real effort was made to speed up services and to place the LYR on a sounder basis to compete more effectively with its neighbours who were threatening to invade its territory.

Manchester suburban services benefited by the construction of several new links. First to open was the Manchester Victoria East Junction–Newton Heath loop, on 4 November 1877. This avoided the steep incline to Miles Platting and gave an easier start for the Yorkshire expresses. At Cheetham Hill Junction, another line, opened to passengers on 1 September 1879, turned northwards through Whitefield to join the former ELR at Radcliffe, south of Bury. In 1916 this was electrified, and it now forms the only route between Manchester and Bury, with the Collyhurst connection to Victoria, opened on 3 October 1904. These lines are to form part of the Piccadilly–Victoria rapid transit system for which Manchester and the surrounding towns keep hoping. Another useful link, from Newton Heath to Oldham Werneth cut out the notorious climb from Middleton Junction and now forms the only route between Manchester and Oldham.

Next to receive attention was the Manchester–Liverpool route. The existing line via Bolton and Wigan made competition with the LNWR and CLC unthinkable. A new four-track main line was built direct from Salford to the Liverpool & Bury line at Hindley with a cut-off south of Wigan to rejoin the former line again at Pemberton. This was opened in sections and finally, on 1 June 1889, they allowed the LYR to establish a fast competing service between the two cities, although it was always a route to test the best locomotives.

By this time the L&Y possessed one of the most modern locomotive works in the country. The former locomotive, carriage and wagon works at Miles Platting had become hopelessly inadequate by the mid 1870s and first to be built was a new carriage works at Newton Heath, opened in 1877. After a search throughout the system a site was found for a new locomotive works at Horwich, about 5 miles (8km) west of Bolton. The works was laid out and begun in 1884 by the locomotive superintendent, William Barton Wright, with John Ramsbottom, former locomotive engineer of the LNWR. Barton Wright resigned in 1886 and was succeeded by J A F Aspinall who completed the erection of the works and then, from 1889, produced a series of locomotive designs, the best of which, the 0–6–0s and 2–4–2 tanks, could still be seen at work in the early 1960s.

In May 1899 the LYR board took the unprecedented step of appointing the chief mechanical engineer, John Aspinall, as its general manager. Under his guidance the LYR moved forward to become one of the most efficient railways in Britain. Passenger services, coaches and stations were modernised, shipping services were extended, and by its connection with the Dearne Valley Railway, completed in 1905–8, and the South Yorkshire Joint Railway, 1909–10, the LYR could carry a large share of the developing Yorkshire coal traffic. Aspinall was also instrumental in the electrification, in 1904, of the Liverpool–Southport line, one of the earliest main-line electrification projects in Britain, and in 1916 of the Manchester–Bury line.

The most progressive locomotive engineer on the LYR was George Hughes who took over at Horwich from Hoy in 1904 and reigned there until he resigned at the age of 60 in 1925. He was one of the earliest engineers to experiment with high-degree superheaters and long travel valves, and in the four-cylinder 4–6–0 of 1921 he produced one of the finest British locomotive designs of that period.

The last section of railway absorbed by the LYR, on 15 July 1897, was the West Lancashire and its connection the Liverpool, Southport & Preston Junction. The West Lancashire, from Southport to Preston, was completed on 16 September 1882. It was a poverty-stricken concern which spent most of its career in the hands of a receiver. So also did the LSPJ, opened in 1887 to connect the WLR at Southport with the Southport & Cheshire Lines Extension, providing an outlet to Liverpool for WLR traffic independently of the LYR. Its motley collection of locomotives was taken into LYR stock, but few survived long.

SOCIAL EFFECTS OF THE L&Y

The influence of the LYR on the social development of the districts it served was enormous. It helped to establish the woollen industry in the West Riding of Yorkshire and the cotton industry in Lancashire. Before the railway both industries flourished on both sides of the Pennines. The LYR, too, did much to concentrate the different processes in various towns, such as cotton spinning in Bolton and Oldham, weaving in the towns around Blackburn, and dyeing, bleaching and finishing in the Rossendale valley and around Rochdale. The movement of all the raw and processed cotton and finished cloth provided the LYR with a heavy freight traffic requiring miles of sidings and hundreds of warehouses. For local deliveries the LYR employed up to 2000 horses and, later, hundreds of motor delivery vans.

Although the immense population employed at the cotton mills lived mostly within walking distance, the LYR made it possible for the better off to live further from their work by providing an intensive service of short distance stopping trains, hence the large proportion of tank locomotives in L&Y stock. It also led to the development of one of the best remembered features of the L&Y, the carriage upholstery in indestructible horsehair fabric.

In the early years of the present century this mobile urban population provided the incentive for the development of electric tramcar routes with cheap fares which drew passengers away from the trains in thousands. This in turn led to the development of light railmotors and, in the conurbations around Liverpool and Manchester, of electrification which, in its turn, drew passengers back to the trains and, by cheap fares, encouraged an ever increasing number to live further out from the towns. These were the people whose descendants are now being punished by heavily increased fares, absorbing a large proportion of their incomes, in overcrowded trains, and whose only alternative is an expensive agonising crawl by road.

For these great hordes of people the only bright hope was the annual week by the sea. During the local 'wakes weeks', when whole towns shut down, the LYR transported hundreds of thousands to and from Blackpool, Fleetwood, Southport, and other resorts on the Lancashire coast, whose very existence had been brought about by the LYR.

For the wealthy mill owners and cotton, wool and textile traders the LYR provided a service of express trains which, considering the nature of the routes abounding in heavy gradients, curves, junctions and short distances between major centres, provided examples of outstanding locomotive performance. It was on these services that the big Aspinall 4–4–2s showed their paces, and speeds between 70 and 80mph (113–129km/h) were common, but as loads grew heavier it was the Hughes superheated 4–6–0s that outshone the rest. Most famous of all the expresses were the 'club trains' between Manchester and Blackpool, mobile businessmen's clubs of an exclusiveness matched nowhere else except possibly on the similar LNW club trains from Manchester to Llandudno.

In the period when the large coal-fired Atlantic liners berthed at Liverpool the LYR handled vast quantities of coal from collieries which it served, handling most of this in the enormous marshalling yard at Aintree. Coal trains of up to 100 wagons would be endlessly trundling to and fro behind Aspinall and Hughes 0–8–0s. One of these trains is illustrated.

Stretching across northern England the LYR naturally connected with the main north-south routes which it crossed. From west to east these were the LNWR, Midland, Great Central, Great Northern, Hull & Barnsley and North Eastern. With all of these it had friendly operating arrangements, but it was with the LNWR that it always worked most closely. In the 1870s attempts were made to amalgamate the two companies but the opposition, chiefly by the Midland, was too great and two amalgamation bills were thrown out. After World War 1 when it was inevitable that the railways would have to amalgamate to survive, the LYR and LNWR entered a new amalgamation bill and from 1 January 1922 the LYR, North London and Dearne Valley Railways became a part of the 'Greater LNWR'. But the LYR did not lose its identity, because its principal officers retained their positions not only in the new combined company, but a year later in the whole of the London, Midland & Scottish Railway. Arthur Watson, formerly an LYR civil engineer and its last general manager, and H. Marriott, assistant general manager, remained in these positions until 1924. The secretary, R C Irwin, became secretary of the LMS, and George Hughes remained CME with his headquarters at Horwich until he resigned in 1925 in protest at the interference by E F C Trench, the former LNWR chief civil engineer.

The LYR system remained practically intact up to Nationalisation on 1 January 1948. The decline began in the 1950s, with further severe pruning in the early 1960s. Today passenger and freight services are but a shadow of those before World War 1, but many people remember the old LYR with affection and for them this collection will provide interesting recollections.

1 Traffic

Above: Another coal train at Horbury hauled by Hughes superheated 0–8–0 No 1577, built in November 1913 and withdrawn as LMS No 12871 in January 1936. With the same bearings as the original Aspinall engines, together with their weight of 66 tons 4cwt in working order, and the immense piston thrusts in the $21\frac{1}{2}$ x 26in (546 x 660mm) cylinders, they soon wore themselves out. The few that remained at the end of 1939, with some other LYR 0–8–0s, were kept in service until after World War 2, but all had gone by the end of 1950. (Vol 3 pp 186–8)
(Locomotive & General Railway Photographs)

Below: For fast passenger work Aspinall designed a class of 4–4–0 with 7ft 3in (2210mm) coupled wheels. Here is an up express at Horbury behind No 1099, built in 1891 and withdrawn in July 1928 as LMS 10155. The tender is one discarded by a Barton Wright 0–6–0 when it was rebuilt into a saddle tank. (Vol 3 pp 137–40)
(Locomotive & General Railway Photographs)

Above: Fleetwood and Blackpool to Rochdale train passing Farington, south of Preston, in the mid 1920s. The train is made up of the 16.00 from Fleetwood, the first two coaches plus cattle truck, which arrived at Poulton at 16.14, where it was joined at 16.27 by the 16.18 from Blackpool Talbot Road to form the 16.30 departure. The train stood at Preston from 17.08 until 17.23 and called at Farington at 17.30. It eventually crawled into Rochdale at 18.53, good enough no doubt for cattle. The engine was LYR 667, built in 1899 and withdrawn in 1950.
(*Locomotive & General Railway Photographs*)

Below: Hughes 4–6–0 No 1525 on a Manchester–York express near Horbury. It is one of 15 engines rebuilt from the original saturated, slide valve type. No 1525 was the last of the original engines, built in 1909 and rebuilt in June 1921. It was withdrawn in November 1934. This photograph was probably taken in 1921–3.
(*Locomotive & General Railway Photographs*)

Above: The last working of a Hughes 4–6–0. No 50455 passes Holgate Bridge, York, on a return Blackpool excursion arranged jointly by the Stephenson Locomotive Society and British Railways on 1 July 1951. The engine was built in 1924 and withdrawn in October 1951.
(*J. P. Wilson*)

Below: A Manchester–Bradford stopping train passing Middleton with 4–6–4 tank No 11112. Ten of these large 4–6–4 tanks were built in 1924. A further 20 which were ordered were built as 4–6–0 tender engines of which No 50455 in the previous photograph was the first. The reason was that there was insufficient suitable work for tank engines of such size and power. (Vol 3 p 196)
(*C. W. Smith*)

Above: Kerr Stuart railmotor No 1, delivered to the LYR from Stoke-on-Trent in 1905. It was the first of two built to a design of Tom Hurry Riches of the Taff Vale Railway. The engines had two boilers and three smokeboxes. They worked at first between Bury and Holcombe Brook and later between Burnley and Colne until the engine units were withdrawn in 1909 and replaced by new ones of George Hughes design. (Vol 3 p 170)
(*British Rail Engineering Ltd*)

Top right: One of the last Aspinall 2–4–2 tanks shunting at Southport on 16 July 1960. This engine, originally LYR No 1313, was built at Horwich in June 1896 and was withdrawn in February 1961. Chapel Street station at Southport was demolished in 1971 and replaced by a small station to handle the only remaining services, to Liverpool and Manchester. (Vol 3 pp 132–3)
(*John Marshall*)

Right: Rebuilt 4–4–0 No 1110 on a Southport–Liverpool train via Ormskirk entering Burscough Bridge station. The engine is one of three Aspinall 4–4–0s rebuilt by George Hughes in 1909 with Schmidt superheaters, Walschaerts valve gear and long-travel piston valves. In this form it gave a remarkable performance, but lubrication troubles led to its reversion to Joy gear and short-travel valves, and consequent inferior performance, after only a few years. (Vol 3 p 139)
(*Locomotive & General Railway Photographs*)

SOUTHPORT
CHAPEL STREET

10192

52181

Left: Manchester to Blackpool and Fleetwood train passing Farington in the mid-1920s behind 7ft 3in 4–4–0 No 10192. This was LYR No 1104 built in 1891. In 1908, along with 1105 and 1110 (shown in the previous photograph) it was also rebuilt with Schmidt superheater, Walschaerts valve gear and long-travel valves, but again lubrication and other troubles led to its further rebuilding in 1914 with a Belpaire boiler with Schmidt superheater and with Joy valve gear. In this form it ran until withdrawn by the LMS in October 1926. (Vol 3 pp 139–40). The train was probably the 15.15 from Manchester with coaches for Blackpool Central, Talbot Road and Fleetwood. The front portion of the train consists of the 60ft (18.288m) long, 9ft (2.743m) wide stock introduced in 1910. (*Locomotive & General Railway Photographs*)

Bottom left: LYR 0–6–0, BR No 52161, performing one of its last duties before withdrawal in October 1960 as a banker for freight trains up the 1 in 47 incline from Manchester Victoria to Miles Platting, photographed at Victoria station on 18 June 1960. This engine, LYR No 1148, was built to Aspinall's design in 1892 and rebuilt with saturated Belpaire boiler in 1912. (Vol 1 pp 136–7) (*John Marshall*)

Below: The last day of steam passenger services on the former Manchester & Leeds main line, on Sunday 31 December 1961. The engine is Jubilee class 4–6–0 No 45698 *Mars* on the 10.05 Liverpool Exchange to York. (*John Marshall*)

Aspinall 4–4–2 on the 14.45 Manchester–Blackpool train on Lostock troughs near Bolton on 15 August 1907. The LYR had ten sets of water troughs. (Vol 3 p 281)
(*National Railway Museum, York*)

2 LOCOMOTIVES

Above: To relieve the engine shortage while the Miles Platting workshops were being reconstructed after the fire of 27 April 1873, the LYR obtained a large number of engines and carriages from the LNWR. These included 86 DX class 0–6–0s, 10 Newton class 2–4–0s, and 5 0–4–0 saddle tanks, the first of which, No 408, is shown here. It was a Ramsbottom design, built at Crewe in March 1872; originally it had no cab, but received one and the 'L&YR 1882' plate when rebuilt in that year. (Vol 1 p 203; Vol 2 pp 79–80) (*British Rail Engineering Ltd*)

Right: Several of the old Barton Wright 0–4–4 tanks and one 0–6–2 tank were used as stationary boilers for carriage heating at various places around the system. These two 0–4–4s were photographed on 27 May 1962 at Blackpool Central where they remained in use until the station closed on 2 November 1964. (Vol 3 p 92) (*John Marshall*)

PALATINE

Above: An unusual view, probably in 1925, at Bank Hall shed (Sandhills) at Liverpool showing superheated 4–6–0, formerly LYR No 1660 built in 1922; and one of the five original saturated 4–6–0s which were not rebuilt and all of which were withdrawn by the end of 1925. (Vol 3 p 193) (*R. W. Hall*)

Below: 0–8–0 No 1427, built in 1902 as a standard Aspinall type, as rebuilt in February 1923 with 28 element superheater Belpaire boiler and side-window cab, carrying the class number 31. In this form it ran until withdrawn in March 1930 as LMS No 12990. (Vol 3 p 188) (*British Railways*)

Above: As mentioned earlier, the WLR and LSPJ contributed an assorted collection of locomotives to the LYR on amalgamation in 1897, but few remained long in LYR stock. This 0–6–0 saddle tank was built by Manning Wardle (No 854) in 1882 and was bought by the WLR for working the Tarleton branch. It was numbered 4 and named *Tarleton*. When the WLR and LSPJ locomotive stocks were combined in 1888 it was renumbered 10. The engine was scrapped in 1897 soon after amalgamation with the LYR. (Vol 3 p 159)
(*British Rail Engineering Ltd*)

Below: Kitson 0–6–2 tank, one of two built in 1887 for the LSPJ, shown lettered WLR after the combination of LSPJ and WLR stock in 1888. They had 5ft 6in (1676mm) coupled wheels and were numbered 3 and 4 on the LSPJ. After amalgamation with the LYR in 1897 they were rebuilt with 5ft 1in (1549mm) wheels, standard with the similar LYR engines. They were scrapped in 1910. (Vol 3 pp 164–7) (*British Rail Engineering Ltd*)

Above: One of two 0–6–2 tanks designed by Harry Pollitt of the Manchester, Sheffield & Lincolnshire Railway, built by Beyer Peacock (Nos 3625–6) in 1894 for the WLR and numbered 8 and 9. In the 1870s and 80s there was a close relationship between the MS&L and the WLR, the MS&L hoping to use the WLR as a means of reaching Blackpool (see Vol 2 pp 167–8). The WLR painted these engines dark purple. No 8 became LYR 1368 and No 9 1369. Both were scrapped in January 1914, although similar engines on the MS&L lasted until the mid 1950s. (Vol 3 p 166) (*British Rail Engineering Ltd*)

3 THE RAILWAY AND ITS ENGINEERING FEATURES

Left: The oldest constituent of the Lancashire & Yorkshire Railway was the Manchester, Bolton & Bury Canal, authorised in 1791 and completed about 1800. In the 1830s the canal company built the Manchester & Bolton Railway, opened on 29 May 1838. At Pendleton near Salford the railway ran beside the canal wall. Pendleton station shown here was opened about August 1843. The photograph was taken just after its closure on 5 December 1966. (Vol 1 p 31) (*John Marshall*)

Above: The Manchester & Leeds Railway was carried over the Rochdale canal near Middleton by this cast iron bridge, built in 1839. It was designed by Thomas Gooch and the girders were cast at Radford's Waterloo Foundry, Manchester. It was replaced in 1904 by a new bridge alongside, of which one abutment may be seen. Photographed on 17 July 1966. (Vol 1 p 44) (*T. A. Fletcher*)

Left: Middleton Junction station on the former Manchester & Leeds main line, photographed on 10 April 1964. It was opened on 31 March 1842, the same day as the branch to Oldham, seen turning off to the right. It was named 'Oldham Junction', then 'Middleton' in August 1842, and 'Middleton Junction' in May 1852. Passenger services to and from Oldham via Middleton Junction were withdrawn on 9 June 1958. The station was closed on 3 January 1966 and was soon demolished completely. The Middleton branch, (see photograph on page 43) diverged to the left beyond the station. (Vol 1 p 59; Vol 2 p 58)
(T. A. Fletcher)

Bottom left: The Manchester & Leeds was built in the grand manner, with magnificent tunnel portals. This is the east end of Elland tunnel, 420yd (384m) long, built in 1840 and photographed on 8 September 1964 from the site of the original Elland station. A second station about 200yd (183m) east was opened on 1 August 1865, and this in turn was replaced by a large island platform opened on 18 February 1894. This was closed on 10 September 1962 and later demolished. (Vol 1 p 45)
(John Marshall)

Below: One of the most fascinating sections of the LYR was the notorious half-mile (0.8km) incline at 1 in 27 on the Manchester & Leeds branch from Middleton Junction to Oldham Werneth, opened on 31 March 1842. It was cable worked, using a balancing system, until about 1854. This photograph was taken on 12 July 1963 from just below Werneth Junction. On the right is a train from Manchester on the later line from Thorpes Bridge Junction, opened on 17 May 1880, itself climbing at 1 in 50. The gradient can be appreciated from the building on the left. The siding entered the works of Platt Bros Ltd. The branch was closed completely on 7 January 1963 and was dismantled in March 1964. (Vol 1 p 58; Vol 2 pp 57–8)
(T. A. Fletcher)

Above: One of the last passenger trains over the branch (on which the author was travelling) clambering up the 1 in 27 into Oldham Werneth on 17 September 1960 behind Belpaire 2–4–2 tank No 50850 (the last one to be withdrawn, in October 1961), assisted in the rear by 0–6–0 No 52271. The chimney top of the 0–6–0 is about level with the rails under the 2–4–2 tank.
(J. A. Cox)

Top right: The south end of Beacon Hill tunnel, 1105yd (1010m), at Halifax carried some unusual decoration. The tunnel was opened on 7 August 1850 and it was interesting in that it was crossed inside by a 'galloway gate', actually an iron tube, connecting coal workings. Photographed on 29 May 1965. (Vol 1 p 251)
(John Marshall)

Right: The north end of Woolley tunnels on the Wakefield–Barnsley branch. With a length of 1745yd (1596m) they were third longest on the LYR. The sidings on the left are on the original line of 1850. The tunnel on the right was opened in 1901. (Vol 1 p 218)
(John Marshall)

Right: The great brick arch of John Hawkshaw, erected in 1849 by McCormick & Holme, to carry the extension of the East Lancashire and LYR joint line over the LNWR Edge Hill–Waterloo branch to Tithebarn Street station, Liverpool. It has a span of 150ft (45.72m) and is 200ft (61m) wide at the near (south) end and 135ft (42m) wide at the far end. It is being used today for the new Liverpool rapid transit line. (Vol 1 p 132) *(John Marshall)*

Below: The south end of Kirkdale tunnels, Liverpool, on 26 April 1968. The original Walton tunnel of 1848, on the right, was 1149yd (1051m) long. The south end was originally near where the footbridge now stands; the north end extended a further 168yd (154m). The widening and alterations were completed in 1904. On the left are the electrified lines used by the Liverpool–Ormskirk trains. (Vol 2 p 99) *(John Marshall)*

Bottom right: Stanier 2–6–4 tank No 42485 on a Blackburn–Manchester train crossing the Croal viaduct at Bolton on 6 October 1960. The viaduct carried the Blackburn Railway over the terminal basin of the Manchester, Bolton & Bury canal, remains of which can be seen in the foreground. The cast iron spans were made by Ogle & Son, Preston, in 1847. (Vol 1 p 182) *(John Marshall)*

Top left: The Croal viaduct on 8 June 1976, now crossing the inner relief road known as St Peter's Way. (*John Marshall*)

Above: One of several wooden overbridges built by the LYR on the Huddersfield–Penistone line, photographed at Berry Brow on 12 May 1963. (Vol 1 p 232) (*John Marshall*)

Left: The iron viaduct, of five 55ft (16.764m) spans, built by Andrew Handyside in 1881 to replace the timber spans of 1846 carrying the ELR Clifton Junction–Bury main line over the Irwell at Radcliffe. The railway was closed on 5 December 1966 and the photograph was taken on 10 June 1967. (Vol 1 p 109) (*John Marshall*)

Above: Lockwood viaduct from the south, looking towards Huddersfield. The full height of the viaduct, 122ft (37m) above the river bed, can be seen in this photograph, taken on 4 June 1966. The viaduct was designed by John Hawkshaw; the resident engineer was John Fraser, later chief engineer of the GNR. The contractors were Miller, Blackie & Shortridge, and it was built in 1847–9. It is 476yd (435m) long and the principal arches have a 30ft (9m) span. (Vol 1 p 229) (*John Marshall*)

Top right: The branch from Windsor Bridge to Salford Docks involved some of the heaviest engineering on the LYR. This view, photographed on 26 June 1963, shows Ellesmere Street tunnel from the mouth of West Park Street tunnel. The branch was opened on 28 March 1898 and was closed on 15 June 1963. (Vol 2 pp 70–3) (*John Marshall*)

Right: Britannia, on the Bacup–Rochdale line in February 1958, the summit of the LYR system, 965ft (294m) above sea level. Passenger services ended on 16 June 1947 and the line remained in a state of semi-disuse until the removal of the junction at Bacup in 1954. Even so, the track was not removed until 1961. On the right an incline led up to Height End and Hall Cowm quarries until closure in 1947. (Vol 2 p 25) (*S. Wolstenholme*)

Right: Manchester Victoria station from the roof of the Co-operative Insurance building, on 28 July 1964. The earliest portion of the station is seen in the top left, while just below are the offices built in 1904–9. In the foreground is the 'fish dock'; above this are the bay platforms and at the top are the through platforms, once covered by an overall roof which was destroyed in World War 2. In the top right can be seen the remains of the old Manchester Workhouse, used as railway offices until, together with the old Hunts Bank offices at the upper left, they were closed when staff was transferred to Rail House, Piccadilly. The old workhouse buildings are now demolished. Rails are now removed from the fish dock and from platforms 1–3, bottom right, and the Bury electric services have been transferred to platforms 4 and 5 to clear a way for the long-hoped-for Picc-Vic underground connection. (Vol 2 pp 58–65) (*John Marshall*)

4 STATIONS

Below: The principal station and the headquarters of the Lancashire & Yorkshire Railway was Manchester Victoria, here seen on 7 July 1968 from the approach to Exchange station. Directly ahead is Hunt's Bank, at the top of which is the station frontage built in 1904–9. To its left, in the centre of the picture, is the original building of 1844 to which a second storey was added shortly afterwards. To the right are the LYR head offices and on the extreme right is the former Palatine Hotel, built in connection with the station in 1844, and now entirely taken over by Chetham's Hospital School of Music. On the left is the long platform connecting Victoria No 11 and the former Exchange No 3. Below, the murky Irk emerges from its long sinuous culvert beneath the station and Walker's Croft, immediately to join the Irwell. (Vol 1 pp 55–8; Vol 2 pp 57–65) (*T. A. Fletcher*)

Bottom right: Hebden Bridge station on the former Manchester & Leeds main line, looking east on 9 May 1965. The platforms are connected by a subway. (*John Marshall*)

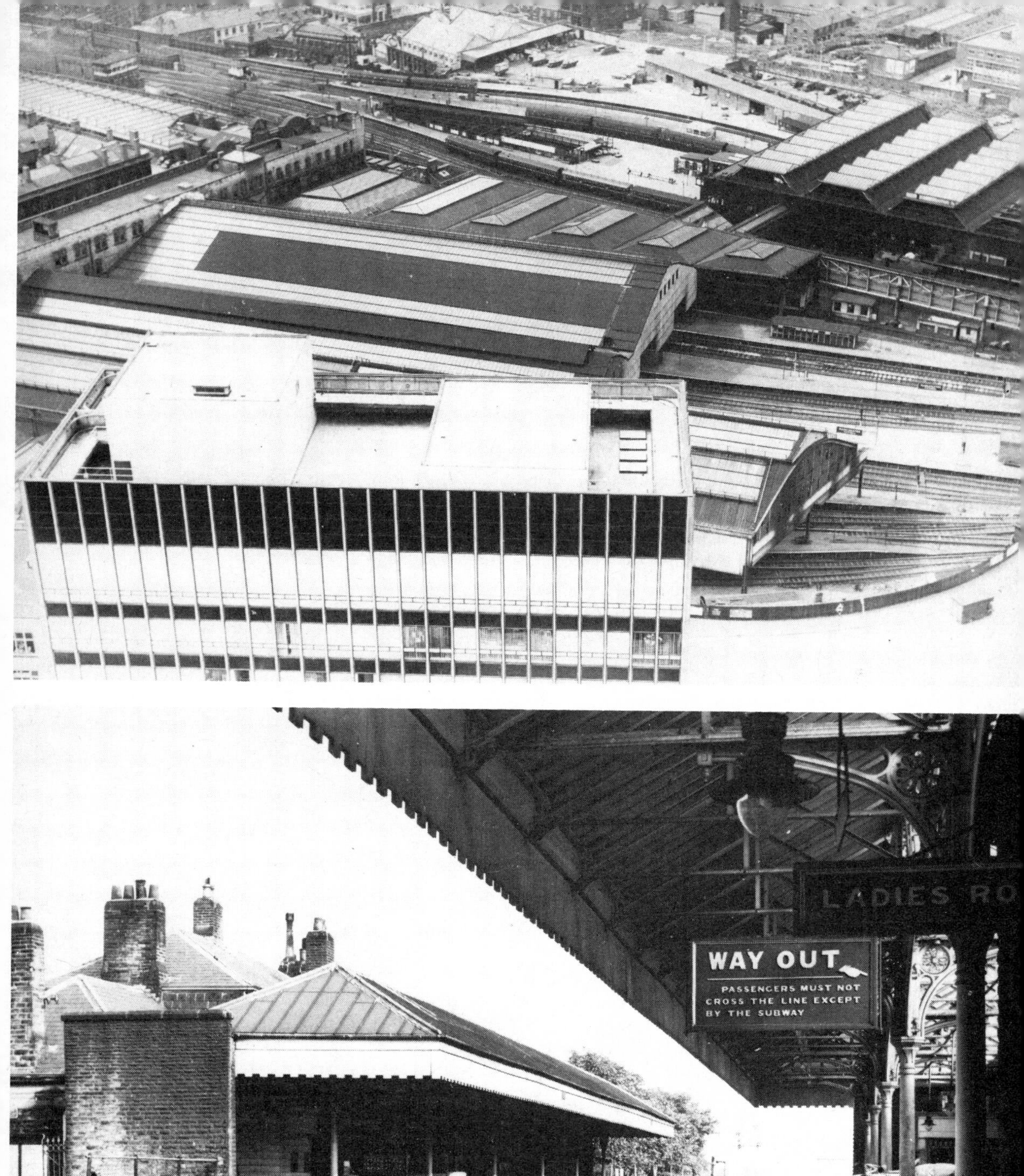

LADIES RO
WAY OUT
PASSENGERS MUST NOT
CROSS THE LINE EXCEPT
BY THE SUBWAY

Above: Blackrod station, 12 July 1968, on the Bolton & Preston Railway, looking towards Preston. It was opened on 4 February 1841 and was known as Blackrod for Horwich until the Horwich branch was opened on 14 February 1870. The branch passes behind the goods shed on the right and trails in beyond the platform. The buildings have now been demolished. (Vol 1 p 78) (*John Marshall*)

Top right: Manchester–Oldham–Rochdale train in Oldham Central station on 3 April 1966. The station was opened on 1 November 1847 as part of the Oldham branch extension from Werneth to Mumps. The last trains stopped there on 16 April 1966 and the station was closed from 18 April. (Vol 2 pp 13–14) (*T. A. Fletcher*)

Right: Skelmersdale station, photographed on 26 October 1912. Note the low platforms and the set of steps. The Ormskirk–Rainford branch of the ELR was opened on 1 March 1858. Passenger services ended on 5 November 1956 and the station was dismantled in 1964–5. All trace of the railway has now gone. (Vol 1 p 146) (*National Railway Museum, York*)

B5
OLDHAM
CENTRAL

SKELMERSDALE

Top left: Entwistle station near the summit of the Blackburn–Bolton line on 17 March 1968, looking towards Blackburn. Originally it was a two-platform station, opened on 1 August 1848, but in 1902–4 when the line here was quadrupled it was rebuilt, the down platform becoming the up and a new down line being laid round the back to form an island station. The new signal box was built at the same time. Today everything has gone except a single track through the straight platform. (Vol 1 pp 181, 197) *(T.A. Fletcher)*

Above: Manchester train at Middleton on 4 May 1963. It was the terminus of a 1$\frac{3}{4}$ mile (2.8km) double-track branch, opened on 5 January 1857. This station was the second and was completed in February 1882. It was unusual among LYR branch termini in having two platforms. Right up to the end the two-car diesel sets would arrive at one platform and then transfer to the other for departure. The photograph was taken during a busy period. Few people were inconvenienced when the passenger service was withdrawn on 7 September 1964; the branch was closed completely on 11 October 1965 and dismantled. (Vol 2 pp 16, 42) *(John Marshall)*

Left: Holmfirth station, a typical LYR single-platform terminus on a double-track branch. It was opened on 1 July 1850, a day of great local celebrations despite torrential rain. Passenger services ended on 2 November 1959 and goods traffic on 3 May 1965 after which the branch was dismantled. (Vol 1 p 232) Photographed on 7 June 1964. *(John Marshall)*

Right: On 16 July 1883 a new station was opened at Fleetwood with an adjoining timber jetty and freight shed. This photograph shows the station concourse and on the right the entrance to the covered passageway to the steamer berth. Trains to and from Manchester and London connected with Belfast steamers until 1928 and Isle of Man steamers until 1961. In that year the jetty was condemned and later demolished. The station was closed on 18 April 1966 and was completely demolished. Train services were cut back to Wyre Dock until that closed on 1 June 1970. (Vol 1 pp 95, 99)
(*British Rail Engineering Ltd*)

Bottom right: The freight shed and quay at Fleetwood in 1924. The ship alongside is either *Duke of Argyll* or *Duke of Cumberland*, both built by Denny in 1909. The ship arrived from Belfast about 05.15 and according to the shadows the time is about 06.30 in mid June. Cargo is being unloaded. Passengers have already disembarked and have left by the 06.05 express to London or the 06.15 express to Manchester, Bradford and Leeds. Both trains included breakfast cars. The Belfast service was transferred to Heysham on 28 April 1928 and the two 'Dukes' were acquired by the Angleterre–Lorraine–Alsace Société Anonyme de Navigation for the Tilbury–Dunkirk service and renamed *Alsacien* and *Picard* respectively (Vol 2 p 183). *Alsacien* was broken up in 1936. *Picard* was sold in November 1936 to the Skenderia Shipping Co who renamed her *Heliopolis*.
(*Locomotive & General Railway Photographs*)

Below: Bacup, where the first station, originally the terminus of the ELR branch, was opened on 1 October 1852. This later station with two platform faces was made necessary by the completion of the branch from Rochdale, opened on 1 December 1881. The photograph, taken from the signal box on 28 July 1962, shows a rail tour train with an Aspinall 0–6–0. The Rochdale service ended on 16 June 1947 and the station was finally closed on 5 December 1966 when the service was cut back to Rawtenstall. (Vol 1 pp 116–17; Vol 2 pp 24–5, 42)
(*John Marshall*)

TO THE STEAMERS

FLEETWOOD CRA
LANCASHIRE & YORKSHI E RAILWA CO

Left: The Fleetwood grain elevator soon after completion in 1883. The 'ship's leg' for extracting grain from ships' holds can be seen on the left. The building measured 300ft (91.44m) long, 90ft (27.43m) wide and 140ft (42.67m) high and contained 143 storage silos each of 200 tons capacity. (Vol 1 p 91) (*British Rail Engineering Ltd*)

Below: The town of Fleetwood was named after its founder, Peter Hesketh Fleetwood (1801–66), who appointed the famous architect Decimus Burton (1800–81) to design the principal buildings including the North Euston Hotel, so named because for a time it formed the northern terminus of the route from Euston, London, to Scotland. Passengers travelled to Fleetwood by train then, after a night at the hotel, continued their journey by sea. The hotel was completed in 1840, and the two lighthouses were first lit on 1 December 1840. (Vol 1 pp 81–2) (*From an old print*)

TO THE GREAT NORTHERN VICTORIA HOTEL
LANCASHIRE & YORKSHIRE RAILWAY
MAGNIFICENT SEA TRIP
HULL TO FLEETWOOD
PENDLETON
LONDON & NORTH WESTERN RAILWAY
LONDON
GREAT CENTRAL RAILWAY
CROSSLEY'S
ECONOMY

Left: Bradford Exchange station, LYR side, on 30 August 1912. The GNR side, on the left, was opened in 1887 and the LYR in May 1888. The two arched roofs were 450ft (137m) long and 100ft (30.5m) span. This station replaced the former inadequate one of 1867 and it was to last for a little over a century. It was last used on 13 January 1973 and a new smaller station was opened, immediately to the south, on 15 January. The entire building was subsequently demolished.

(*National Railway Museum, York*)

Bottom left: The West Lancashire Railway, from Southport to Preston, and its associate the Liverpool, Southport & Preston Junction from Southport to the Southport & Cheshire Lines Extension at Hillhouse Junction, were poverty stricken concerns which spent almost their entire existence in the hands of a receiver until amalgamation with the LYR in 1897. Apart from Southport and Preston they served a sparsely populated district and traffic was always light.

Hesketh Bank station was typical of several between Southport and Preston. The photograph, looking towards Preston probably in early LYR days, shows few people waiting for the trains, for there were few houses in the vicinity, yet surprisingly the station survived until closure of the line on 7 September 1964. (Vol 1 pp 160–74)

(*From an old postcard*)

Below: The only photograph in this collection of a railway under construction is this one showing the temporary drawbridge across the Douglas at Hesketh Bank during the construction of the West Lancashire Railway in 1881. The permanent bridge, illustrated in Vol 1 p 143, was completed and the line opened on 18 May 1882. (Vol 1 p 165)

Above: The WLR station in Lower Fishergate, Preston, showing the timber platform as cut back after closure. The station was opened on 16 September 1882. It had a 400ft (122m) long platform covered by a roof 240ft (73m) long. After the WLR was amalgamated with the LYR in 1897 the Whitehouse west–north curve was built and opened on 16 July 1900 on which date the Fishergate station was closed and the Southport trains ran into the ELR section of the joint station. Fishergate remained in use for goods traffic until 26 January 1965. (Vol 1 pp 166, 172)
(*Locomotive & General Railway Photographs*)

Left: One of the rare relics of the LSPJ which survived, and may still exist, was this clock, photographed on 10 August 1962 in the signalbox at Werneth, Oldham. The signalbox can be seen in the photograph on p 30. It was closed on 22 May 1967 and demolished. (*T. A. Fletcher*)

5 JUNCTIONS

Below: One third of the 738 signalboxes owned or jointly owned by the LYR controlled junctions; many of more than two routes. One of the biggest junctions was Crow Nest near Hindley, here photographed on 11 April 1968. In the centre is the first line on the scene, from Lostock Junction near Bolton to Liverpool, opened on 20 November 1848. Next came the line on the left from Blackrod, opened on 15 July 1868. Last came the four-track main line from Manchester, opened on 1 October 1888. Notice the switch diamonds. The fast lines on the right were taken out of use on 6 September 1965 and the Blackrod branch was closed on 9 September 1968. Compare this with the recent photograph from the same place. *(John Marshall)*

Right: The interior of the Crow Nest Junction signalbox of 1888, probably about 1902.
(*British Rail Engineering Ltd*)

Bottom right: Rainford Junction, on 26 August 1964. Straight ahead is the line to Liverpool. Left if the former St Helens Railway, (LNWR) opened on 1 February 1858 and closed to passengers on 18 June 1951 and to freight on 6 July 1964. On the right is the former ELR branch to Skelmersdale and Ormskirk, opened on 1 March 1858, closed to passengers on 5 November 1956 and to freight on 16 November 1961. The ELR and LNWR made an end-on junction at the bridge in the background. In the top right corner can be seen the signalbox at Bushey Lane Junction. (Vol 1 p 146) (*John Marshall*)

Below: Crow Nest Junction photographed on 26 May 1976. All that remains are the lines from Lostock Junction and the slow lines from Manchester, controlled by a new signalbox. One of the switch diamonds has survived.
(*John Marshall*)

Top left: Bolton West Junction on 28 April 1968. The awning in front of the station, built in 1904, was demolished on 20–24 May. In 1968–9 the iron bridge of 1880 carrying Trinity Street was completely replaced by a concrete structure. Subsequently the track layout was much simplified as shown in the next photograph. The junction was laid out in 1904 and was controlled from the Bolton West box, just off the picture to the left, by the first electro-pneumatic signalling system in Britain, which is still in use. (Vol 1 pp 196–7; Vol 2 pp 242–3)
(*John Marshall*)

Above: Darwen–Blackpool excursion on Johnson Street Fork connecting the Blackburn and Preston lines north of Bolton station, photographed on 22 May 1961 from almost the same place as the two photographs of West Junction. The locomotive is Crab 2–6–0 No 42729, built at Horwich in 1927. The fork was opened on 26 March 1888. It never carried a regular passenger service and was latterly used only by coal trains from Bullfield sidings to the power station at Halliwell. The last passenger train to use it was a special on 18 May 1968 after which the curve was closed and dismantled. (Vol 1 p 189)
(*John Marshall*)

Left: Bolton West Junction on 1 August 1976 showing the new Trinity Street bridge and the simplified track layout. Straight ahead is the line to Manchester, opened on 29 May 1838; to the right is the Preston line opened as far as Rawlinson Bridge near Chorley on 4 February 1841, and to the left is the Blackburn line opened on 12 June 1848.
(*John Marshall*)

6 ACCIDENTS AND CRANES

Right: The LYR was by no means free from accidents. Besides some serious smashes involving severe loss of life there were numerous derailments and pile-ups, and the breakdown gangs were kept busy; in fact LYR gangs achieved a reputation of being among the smartest in England. This is the accident at King William sidings, Bromley Cross, on 5 February 1889. An engine from Miles Platting was standing on the up line after shunting wagons into the sidings, protected by the home signal. A 15-wagon coal train from Blackburn, approaching down the 1 in 70, was unable to stop on the wet rails. When a collision appeared inevitable the crews leapt clear and the Miles Platting fireman managed to stop a carriage and two horses coming down the road just before the crash. The Blackburn engine, Barton Wright 0–6–0 No 136 (1879) was derailed and with its tender fell into the road with four wagons on top of it. No-one was injured, but it was Sunday 10 February before the engine and tender could be hoisted back onto the rails by a crane. Five years later the engine was rebuilt into a saddle tank, and it was withdrawn as BR 51379 in April 1955, aged 75. (Vol 1 p 181; Vol 3 p 233)
(*British Rail Engineering Ltd*)

Left: The Horwich fire train, complete with Merryweather steam fire engine and coach for firemen and equipment, photographed on 30 May 1914 at Horwich. It was maintained like a breakdown train for immediate dispatch to any part of the system, though one can easily imagine that a fire at Goole would have burned itself out by the time the train arrived. However, the train was maintained well into the LMS period before it was conceded that local fire brigades could deal with any but the most remote lineside fires more effectively. (*National Railway Museum, York*)

Above: Derailment at Mirfield on 28 March 1895, showing the old Mirfield 5 ton hand crane in use. The locomotive is a Ramsbottom DX 0–6–0, one of those supplied to the LYR by the LNWR in 1871–4. In January 1922 an identical accident happened to 0–8–0 No 1365 in exactly the same place. *(British Rail Engineering Ltd)*

Below: Six passengers and one railwayman were killed on 15 July 1903 when 2–4–2 tank No 670 derailed on a sharp curve near Waterloo station while working a Liverpool–Southport express. The cause was breakage of the right trailing coupled wheel spring buckle.

Above: Occasionally LYR gangs had to deal with accidents to privately-owned engines. On 22 April 1907 the 0–4–0 tank *Greenacres*, one of twelve built from 1866 by Daniel Adamson & Co of Hyde Junction for Platt Bros of Oldham, ran away down the siding alongside the 1 in 27 Werneth incline and crashed into Walsh Street. There were no injuries. Here it is being recovered by the then brand new 30 ton crane from Newton Heath.

Above: Newton Heath 30 ton breakdown crane built in 1906 by Cowans Sheldon, Carlisle (No 2954). The photograph is dated 28 March 1907. During World War 1 this crane was sent to France and was afterwards returned to the LYR and transferred to Wakefield, then in 1925 to Leeds, and to Grimesthorpe in 1931.
(British Rail Engineering Ltd)

Below: Sandhills 35 ton crane built by Craven Bros, Manchester, in 1911 (No C9158). It was the largest crane on the LYR and was used all over the system, appearing at Penistone in February 1916 after the collapse of the viaduct (Vol 1 pp 162, 243). The crane was known as 'The Maggie' and remained at Sandhills (later Bank Hall) until the shed closed on 22 October 1966 when it was transferred to Edge Hill. It was withdrawn the following year.
(British Rail Engineering Ltd)

7 HORWICH WORKS

Below: Horwich Works drawing office. Several famous locomotive engineers including Gresley and Maunsell received part of their training in this office, where complete design work was carried out for every type of locomotive built at Horwich from the 2–4–2 tanks of 1889 to the LMS 2–6–0s of 1927 and for much ancillary equipment. Subsequently much of the design work was undertaken here on various LMS and BR locomotives. (Vol 2 p 215) (*British Rail Engineering Ltd*)

Overleaf: No 5 erecting shop at Horwich showing Barton Wright 4–4–0s under repair about 1888–90. On the left is 4–4–0 No 681, withdrawn in 1896. Centre right is a Ramsbotton DX class 0–6–0. The overhead cranes were then operated by 'running ropes' seen on the right, powered by a steam engine at one end of the shop. Vol 2 pp 210–18) (*National Railway Museum, York*)

HETHERINGTON & Co MANCHESTER 1886

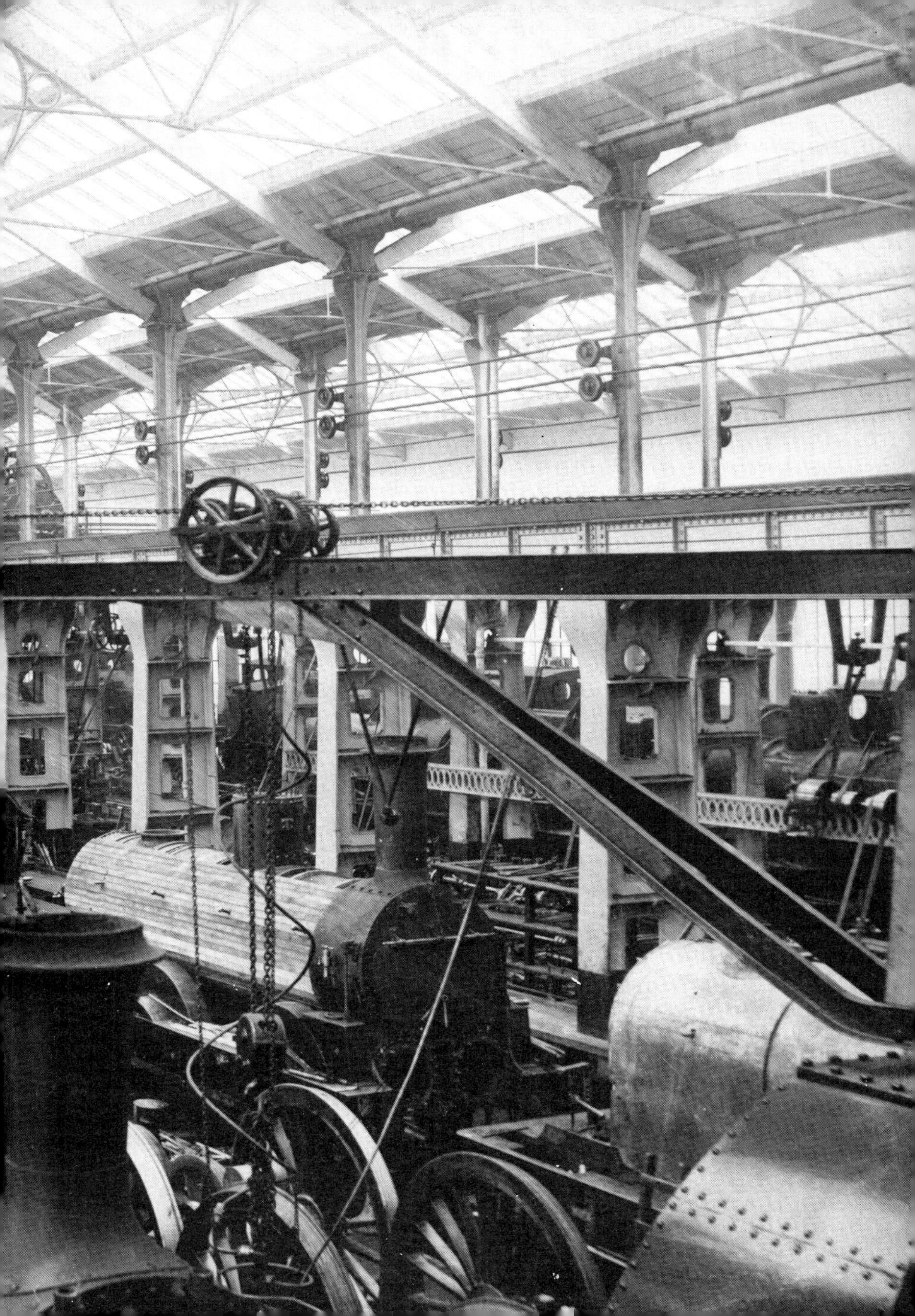

Left: Horwich wheel shop, in the days before the shafting and belts were replaced by separate motors for each machine. (Vol 2 p 221) *(British Rail Engineering Ltd)*

Overleaf: Horwich boiler shop showing the 18in gauge tramway and machine for bending boiler plates. The shop was 439ft (134m) long and 111ft (34m) wide. (Vol 2 p 217–18) *(National Railway Museum, York)*

Bottom left: The signal shop at Horwich in which the LYR manufactured all its own signalling equipment. Much of the workshop equipment remains in use today. (Vol 2 p 221) *(British Rail Engineering Ltd)*

Below: Locomotives under repair at Horwich in 1910, including Aspinall 0–6–0 and 4–4–0, Hughes 0–8–2 tank and Aspinall 4–4–2. (Vol 2 p 218) *(British Railways)*

Above: Horwich paint shop in August 1919. It took about three weeks to paint a new LYR engine. First, all rust was removed by scouring with sandstone and washing with turpentine. Two coats of oil and white lead were applied, followed by enamel filling worked on with trowels, hollow places being filled by thicker stopping. After a thin coat of black stain to guide rubbing down to a smooth surface, the first coat of paint was applied, white lead and common black mixed with boiled linseed oil and liquid terebene. A second coat of best drop ivory black and a third coat of ivory black mixed with varnish were put on, followed by the fixing of the company's arms, transfers, and lining out. The work was finished with three coats of varnish. Buffer beams and insides of frames were given three coats of vermilion and varnish. Wheels, frames and smokebox had a coat of drop ivory black and two coats of Japan black. (Vol 2 p 220) *(National Railway Museum, York)*

Below: As in other railway works, hours of work were long and hard at Horwich; but there was still time for recreation. Here is the works band, photographed on 14 November 1908, in front of the bandstand erected in June 1907 in the recreation ground opposite the works by Henry Yates Thompson, a prominent LYR director. The band gave frequent performances here in the spring and summer. *(National Railway Museum, York)*

Above: Fern Bank, Chorley New Road, Bolton, the home of Aspinall during his period as chief mechanical engineer at Horwich, 1886–99. Photographed in June 1968. (Vol 2 pp 213–19) (*John Marshall*)

Below: Wingfield, Victoria Road, Heaton, Bolton, where George Hughes lived from 1904–25 while he was CME at Horwich. In the extensive garden he was able to indulge his love of horticulture. It was only a short walk down to Chorley New Road where he would board a Bolton tram for his three-mile journey to the works. He would happily sit beside one of the workers or apprentices for a friendly chat on the way. (*John Marshall*)

Above: In 1908 George Hughes fitted up a four-wheeled guard's van as a mobile lecture room, furnishing it with models of valve gears, brakes, injectors, etc, drawings and diagrams, and a library of technical books. The car toured various locomotive depots where lectures would be given by senior technical staff to mutual improvement classes, outside working hours. (Vol 3 p 177)
(*British Rail Engineering Ltd*)

Top right: The interior of the Horwich dynamometer car after rebuilding in 1929 when steam heating was fitted. (Vol 3 p 186)
(*British Railways*)

Below: In 1911 Hughes visited Belgium where he was greatly impressed by Flamme's dynamometer car. On his return to Horwich he designed one for the LYR. This photograph is dated 11 January 1912, although the car was not completed until later in that year when it went into use on coal trains between Aintree and Goole in connection with the proposed 2–10–0 design, again based on a Flamme engine. (Vol 3 p 186)
(*British Rail Engineering Ltd*)

Bottom right: Newton Heath carriage shop photographed on 25 November 1915, showing steel and wooden coaches being erected (Vol 2 p 208)
(*National Railway Museum, York*)

8 ELECTRIFICATION

Above: Formby power station on the Liverpool–Southport electric line. It was built in 1904 by Thomas Croft & Sons of Preston to designs by Dick, Kerr. It was in use until 1946. Photographed on 1 May 1966. (Vol 2 p 159) (*John Marshall*)

Above: Yates & Thom, Blackburn, cross-compound Corliss type engines and alternators in Formby power station on the Liverpool–Southport line. The flywheels were 22ft diameter and the alternators had an output of 1500 kW. They were replaced by turbines in 1927. The power station was closed down in 1946 when power was obtained from the National Grid. (Vol 2 p 159)
(*British Rail Engineering Ltd*)

Below: A seven-car train of Liverpool–Southport 1904 electric stock outside the Meols Cop workshops at Southport. The workshops were completed in 1913. The cars measured 60ft (18.288m) long and 10ft (3.048m) wide, and were the widest on any British standard gauge railway. Even the widest GWR broad gauge coaches were no more than 10ft 6in wide. (Vol 2 pp 160–7)
(*English Electric Co Ltd*)

Above: Meols Cop electric car works, Southport, photographed in July 1947. The works were built in 1913 and were closed on 14 February 1970. (Vol 2 p 167) (*C. E. Box*)

Below: An electric motor coach from Aintree at Gladstone Dock station, on the North Mersey branch near Liverpool, on 9 September 1914. The station was opened two days earlier to serve workers at the new Gladstone dock. However, Seaforth Sands station on the Liverpool Overhead Railway, seen in the background, proved more convenient, and Gladstone Dock station was closed on 7 July 1924. (Vol 2 p 168) (*National Railway Museum, York*)

Above: Electric locomotive No 1 designed by Hughes on a 2–4–2 tank chassis in 1910–11 and completed in 1912 for shunting at Aintree yard where it worked for about seven years. For its use, overhead catenary was erected to supply direct current at 600V. About 1919 it was transferred to Meols Cop electric car shops at Southport where it ended its days until withdrawal in 1920. (Vol 3 p 184) (*British Railways*)

Below: To provide additional electric trains for handling the vast crowds of people travelling between Liverpool Exchange and Aintree, as many as 13 000 on Grand National day, the LYR coupled a power car to each end of a string of ten six-wheeled coaches, connecting them by cables along the roofs. These trains were first used in March 1907 following completion of the electrification to Aintree via the North Mersey branch in June 1906. Photographed at Aintree on 10 April 1907. (Vol 2 p 166) (*British Railways*)

Above: For the through service between Southport and the Liverpool Overhead Railway to Dingle, begun on 2 February 1906, the LYR ordered twelve light-weight cars of which this, No 1005, was one. It was built by Dick, Kerr at Preston and carried 20 first-class and 50 third-class passengers. During World War 1 they were transferred to the Southport–Crossens shuttle service on which they ran until withdrawn in 1946. (Vol 2 p 165)
(*British Rail Engineering Ltd*)

Below: Battery-electric locomotive No 2 built at Horwich in 1917–18 shunting wagons at Clifton Junction power station. It worked at Clifton until the power station was closed, after which it worked in Scotland. (Vol 3 pp 191–2) (*National Railway Museum, York*)

Above: A rare photograph of an electric train at Holcombe Brook. The train is a standard LYR set built for the 1200V Manchester–Bury system. The Holcombe Brook branch was opened on 6 November 1882. In 1913 it was used for an experiment by Dick, Kerr of Preston in high-voltage dc electrification using an overhead system at 3600V. In 1916, when the experiment was concluded, the branch was re-electrified at 1200V dc as an extension of the Manchester–Bury system, using the same side-contact third rail conductor but without the earthed centre rail. The LYR electric trains began running on 29 March 1918. They were withdrawn on 25 March 1951, when the equipment needed renewal, and the branch reverted to steam operation until its closure to passengers on 5 May 1952. Goods trains terminated at Tottington from 2 May 1960 and the branch was closed completely on 19 August 1963. (Vol 2 pp 67–8; 177). The station site is now a shopping centre.
(*Locomotive & General Railway Photographs*)

9 PASSENGER COACHES

Below: Family saloon No 100, the last four-wheeled first-class carriage to be built by the LYR, about 1878. Length 27ft 6in (8.38m) over body, wheelbase 15ft 6in (4.724m)
(*British Rail Engineering Ltd*)

3rd
3rd
1422
3rd
L.Y.R
3rd
3rd

3rd
3rd
830
3rd
L.Y.R
3rd
3rd

901
L.Y.R

Top left: The last four-wheeled carriage to be built for the LYR, in 1878, photographed on 19 April 1912. It measured 27ft 6in (8.38m) over body, 8ft (2.438m) wide, with a wheelbase of 15ft 6in (4.724m). It weighed 9 tons 15cwt. (Vol 3 p 110) (*British Rail Engineering Ltd*)

Above: Invalid carriage, designed by F. Attock and built in 1887. Dimensions are the same as No 830. (*British Rail Engineering Ltd*)

Centre left: Third-class carriage No 830, designed by F. Attock in 1883, incorporating 'Grover's flexible wheelbase'. The new livery of lower panels in lake, and upper in brown was adopted for all new stock from 29 November 1881. Length over buffers 35ft 7in (10.846m), body 32ft (9.754m), wheelbase 20ft (6.096m). (Vol 3 pp 109, 111, 115) (*British Rail Engineering Ltd*)

Below: A train of 1907 stock photographed at Horwich on 13 April 1908 with a Belpaire 2–4–2 tank, still in the livery established by Hoy in 1902. From 1905–9 the Carriage & Wagon Superintendent at Newton Heath was J. P. Crouch. (*National Railway Museum, York*)

FIRST CLASS
L.Y.R
THIRD CLASS
FIRST CLASS
L.Y.R
FIRST CLASS
196
L.Y.R
THIRD CLASS
L.Y.R

Top and centre left: Three of the eight coaches built in 1913 for the new service introduced on 24 December between Manchester and Southport. The bogies were a new LYR standard pattern with 3ft 6in (1067mm) wheels and a wheelbase of 10ft (3.048m) spaced at 38ft (11.582m) centres. The coaches were 56ft (17.069m) long over bodies, 59ft 7in (18.161m) over buffers and 9ft (2.743m) wide. They were lit by gas, and most elaborate precautions were taken against fire following the report on the tragedies at Hawes Junction and Ais Gill on the Midland Railway. Electric lighting became standard from 1914. The photographs are dated October 1913.
(*British Railways*)

Bottom left: An early directors' saloon attached to former ELR 2–4–0 No 640 *Fire King*. This engine was built by Walker Bros of Bury in May 1849 and was rebuilt with cab in 1870. The photograph was taken at Horwich, probably during an inspection of the unfinished works.
(*British Railways*)

Below: Directors' saloon No 1, built in 1878. This has an interesting history. When it was replaced by a new larger saloon in 1908 it was rebuilt at Newton Heath into a bogie vehicle and renumbered 2, and was used as an engineers' saloon, becoming LMS 10772. It remained in use in Lancashire until 1948 when it was moved to Inverness where it remained until withdrawn in 1965. It was then purchased privately and today is preserved on the Keighley & Worth Valley Railway. The body measured 34ft 10in (10.617m) long. (*British Rail Engineering Ltd*)

10 GOODS YARDS AND VEHICLES

Above: The electric cantilever crane, built in 1907 by Muskers of Liverpool, for handling timber in the North Mersey yard. It had a transverse span of 172ft (52.426m). Beyond is the Liverpool Overhead Railway. The crane was sold to a demolition contractor on 10 September 1952. (Vol 1 p 160; Vol 2 p 103) *(British Rail Engineering Ltd)*

Below: The 1 in 27 incline from Salford Low Level goods yard to Oldfield Road, opened in April 1867, and photographed on 22 December 1966. The yard was closed on 3 April 1967 and all trace of the incline was removed. (Vol 2 pp 43–5) *(John Marshall)*

Above: The warehouse and part of the timber gantry at Oldham Werneth goods yard, on 22 March 1964. They were built by Thomas Wrigley in 1887–8. The yard was closed on 10 October 1966. (Vol 2 p 37) (*T. A. Fletcher*)

Below: Astley Bridge terminus, Bolton, opened on 15 October 1877. The passenger service lasted only until 1 October 1879, but the terminus remained in use as a coal depot until 1959. Photographed on 27 June 1960. (Vol 1 p 198) (*John Marshall*)

Above: 0–6–0 saddle tank shunting at Halliwell on the Astley Bridge branch at Bolton on 14 May 1960. Halliwell has survived as the principal Bolton goods yard. (Vol 1 p 198) *(John Marshall)*

Below: The old LYR branch terminus at Stalybridge, opened on 5 October 1846 as the Ashton, Stalybridge & Liverpool Junction Railway. It became part of the LYR when that company was formed by the Act of 9 July 1847. The passenger station was closed finally from 2 April 1917 when LYR trains began running into the adjacent GCR station. The goods warehouse was built in 1884. Goods traffic finished on 27 February 1965 and the buildings were demolished. Photographed on 3 April 1963. (Vol 1 pp 63; 226) *(John Marshall)*

Above: Aintree sorting sidings from the North Mersey branch on 13 June 1964, shortly before closure. The sidings covered 34½ acres (14ha) with over 18 miles (29km) of track, and were opened in 1886. (Vol 2 pp 87–8)
(*John Marshall*)

Below: One of the 10 ton goods brake vans introduced in 1889. The bodies were covered in iron sheeting 'up to 4ft wide' (1.219m) to increase weight and to exclude draughts. This van was marked to indicate that it carried a fire extinguisher. (Vol 3 p 121)
(*British Rail Engineering Ltd*)

Above: An early type of cattle wagon, 15ft 6in (4.724m), without screw couplings or continuous brake. A later type, introduced in 1897–8, was so equipped. (Vol 3 p 122)
(*British Rail Engineering Ltd*)

Below: In 1901 Hoy introduced three types of 30 ton bogie goods vehicles, high-sided and low-sided wagons and a covered van, for Goole shipping traffic in anticipation of the purchase of the Goole Steam Shipping Co fleet in 1905. The swivelling bogies were designed to enable the wagons to turn through 90 degrees on ordinary wagon turntables as shown in this photograph. They had vacuum brakes with special connections to the bogies. (Vol 3 p 122) (*British Rail Engineering Ltd*)

Above: Covered goods van, tare weight 7 tons 7cwt, length 21ft 6in (6.553m), showing the new 'L Y' lettering introduced in 1902–3. The wagons were painted dark grey with lettering in white. Photographed on 3 June 1910. (*British Rail Engineering Ltd*)

Below: Gunpowder van, built in 1905. It was built of steel, lined in pine, with a 2ft (0.610m) high additional lining of sheet lead. (*British Rail Engineering Ltd*)

L
Y
FORMBY POWER HOUSE
30790
GUARD
WIGAN
28016
20.5.1

117
L.Y.R
3rd

Top left: Hopper wagon, tare weight 8 tons 11cwt, built in 1905 for coal to Formby power station on the Liverpool–Southport electric line. (Vol 3 p 123)
(*British Rail Engineering Ltd*)

Centre left: A 20 ton six-wheeled brake van with oak-framed body covered with steel plates. It had a steel channel underframe ballasted with cast iron. Although built in 1905 the van carries the circle and triangle badge standard on LYR goods stock until 1902–3 when the large letters 'L Y' were adopted. (Vol 3 p 123)
(*British Rail Engineering Ltd*)

Bottom left: Horse box, tare weight 7 tons 14cwt, used mainly for Aintree race traffic.
(*British Rail Engineering Ltd*)

11 MISCELLANY

Below: LYR parcels van and a Hansom cab at Sowerby Bridge station. The station was built in 1876 in the angle formed by the Ripponden branch when it was expected that this would form part of a new main line. (Vol 2 p 109)
(*British Railways*)

Above: Sentinel steam lorry and trailer loaded with bales of cotton outside Oldham Mumps station on 20 March 1919. (*National Railway Museum, York*)

Below: LYR motor lorry No 1 rebuilt from the Commer bus, No 3, at Horwich about 1910. It had a 36hp engine. The lorry was scrapped in 1920. (Vol 2 p 241) (*British Rail Engineering Ltd*)

Above: Motor lorry No 7 dating from about 1910. By the end of 1921 the LYR had 537 goods and parcels motor vehicles. (Vol 2 p 240) (*British Rail Engineering Ltd*)

Left: LYR boundary stone at The Oaks, Bolton, 10 May 1964. These stones marked the boundary of LYR land all around the system. Width 10in (254mm), thickness 6in (152mm), lettering 3½in (89mm) high. (*John Marshall*)

Below: Cast iron gate notice measuring 23¼in (590mm) × 20½in (520mm). These, together with trespassing notices, were cast in the foundry at Horwich. (*John Marshall*)

LANCASHIRE & YORKSHIRE
RAILWAY
NOTICE
ANY PERSON WHO SHALL NOT SHUT AND FASTEN THIS GATE AFTER PASSING THROUGH IT IS LIABLE TO A PENALTY NOT EXCEEDING FORTY SHILLINGS AND WILL BE PROSECUTED FOR THE OFFENCE
LOOK BOTH UP AND DOWN THE LINE BEFORE YOU CROSS
BY ORDER

Above: Many LYR stations had built-in mosaic signs. This was at Chapel Street station, Southport, now demolished. Photographed on 3 May 1970. (*John Marshall*)

Right: A typical LYR platform ticket machine, at St Lukes, Southport. Could this have collected enough old pennies to cover the cost of its manufacture? The 'art nouveau' windows are typical of the period when the new station at St Lukes Junction was built; it was opened in June 1902. The beautifully dressed stonework is a tribute to E. Taylor, the contractor. (*British Rail Engineering Ltd*)

Overleaf: The only LYR engine shed included here is this view of Lower Darwen, on 25 July 1964. It was an example of the standard pattern introduced by Barton Wright and was opened on 3 September 1881. It was numbered 25 in the LYR shed list. It was closed on 14 February 1966 and the site was completely cleared. On the left is the line to Bolton. (*John Marshall*)

Above: Manchester Victoria luggage transporter, built by Mather & Platt, Salford, in 1898–9. The driver's seat shown was later replaced by one which gave greater freedom of movement. It remained in use until the station was bombed in the early 1940s. Vol 2 p 63)
(*British Rail Engineering Ltd*)

Below: LYR poster advertising shipping services from Goole, photographed on 7 May 1911. All the ships are illustrated. (Vol 2 pp 186–8)
(*National Railway Museum, York*)

Zeebrugge Route via Hull

LANCASHIRE & YORKSHIRE RAILWAY

IRWELL
MERSEY
UNITY
EAST COAST STEAMERS FLAG
MELLIFONT
BERLIN
HUMBER
FRANKFORT
DOUGLAS
RAWCLIFFE
SALTMARSHE
NIDD
EMDEN
WHARFE
HODDER

THE LANCASHIRE & YORKSHIRE Rly Co's EAST COAST FLEET OF STEAMERS CONVEY MERCHANDISE TO & FROM THE CONTINENT VIA GOOLE

CONTINENTAL PORTS	DAYS OF SAILINGS FROM GOOLE	TO GOOLE
AMSTERDAM	WEDNESDAY & SATURDAY.	TUESDAY & SATURDAY.
ANTWERP	MONDAY, WEDNESDAY & SATURDAY.	TUESDAY, THURS & SAT.
BRUGES	SATURDAY.	WEDNESDAY.
COPENHAGEN	WEDNESDAY.	THURSDAY.
DELFZIEL	TUESDAY.	SATURDAY.
DUNKIRK	TUESDAY.	SATURDAY.
GHENT (DIRECT)	WEDNESDAY & SATURDAY.	WEDNESDAY & SATURDAY.
HAMBURG	MON, WED, THURS & SAT.	MON, WED, FRI & SAT.
ROTTERDAM	MONDAY, WEDNESDAY & SAT.	TUESDAY, THURSDAY & SAT.

GOOLE THE MOST INLAND PORT ON THE EAST COAST OF ENGLAND. THE STEAMERS RUN IN DIRECT CONNECTION WITH THE LANCASHIRE & YORKSHIRE RY Co's TRAIN SERVICES TO & FROM ALL PORTS. MERCHANDISE IS TRANSHIPPED DIRECT TO & FROM WAGGONS ALONGSIDE STEAMERS. ALL INFORMATION AS TO RATES &c MAY BE OBTAINED FROM Mr H. MARRIOTT, GOODS MANAGER, Victoria Station, MANCHESTER or Mr G.W. WINTERBOTTOM, Steamship Offices, GOOLE. Telegraphic Address "DESPATCH, GOOLE".

DERWENT
DON
LIBERTY
HEBBLE
EQUITY
SPEN
DEARNE
CALDER
AIRE
ALTONA